Kevin Cloud
chippewa boy in the city

by Carol Ann Bales

Reilly & Lee Books · Chicago

This book is dedicated to two grandmothers:
Mrs. Vivian Cloud and Mrs. Katie Schierbaum.

The author wishes to express her appreciation to David Anderson, Jerry Fryer,
Valerie McLenighan, Dolores Nathanson, and the Cloud family for their special
assistance and to acknowledge the aid and advice of Albert Cobe, a Chippewa born in
a birchbark wigwam in Wisconsin just a few years after the last confrontation
between the Chippewa and occupying U.S. soldiers.

Published by Reilly & Lee Books, a division of Henry Regnery Company
114 West Illinois Street, Chicago, Illinois 60610
Library of Congress Catalog Number 79—183833
Printed in the United States of America

To the Reader

Long before white men came to this country from Europe, the people of the Chippewa tribe lived near the Upper Great Lakes. This land had been their home for hundreds of years. The Chippewa had learned many things about living on their land and about living together.

They taught some of the things that they had learned to the white men. They taught the white men how to live on the land—what food to grow, how to make canoes and snowshoes, and how to travel in them.

The first white men came from France. They brought with them new things that the Chippewa had never seen before. The Chippewa traded beaver furs to the Frenchmen in return for food and some of these new things—metal traps for hunting, iron kettles, glass beads, and guns.

More and more white men began to move into the land of the Chippewa. Some of the things they brought were not good for the Indians— rum and new diseases. The food of the Chippewa—deer, moose, bear, and reindeer—became scarce. The demand for beaver furs came to an end. The Chippewa no longer had a way of buying the new things that they had come to need.

Life became harder for the Chippewa. They were forced to live on reservations, which the white men promised would be Indian land forever. White soldiers were sent to run the reservations, and some of them treated the Indians badly. Fights broke out, but in the end the Chippewa lost.

The reservations were small. The Chippewa had been hunters, but to live on the reservations they had to become farmers. They were not permitted to practice their religion. Chippewa children were sent away from their families to white boarding schools. There they were forbidden to speak the Indian language. They were taught the ways of the white men.

Some years have passed. The Chippewa have tried to keep the ways of their ancestors, but they have been forced to change in many ways. Large numbers of Indian families have moved from the reservations to big cities to find work. It is hard for many Indians to live in the cities, but there are not enough jobs on the reservations.

When you read this book, you will see that Kevin is a lot like you. But you also will see, if you read carefully, that Kevin knows about some things and does some things that have been passed down to him from a long time ago.

This makes him special. There are many such people in our country because there are many people who have had special ideas and ways of doing things passed down to them from their parents, grandparents, and great-grandparents. Perhaps you have, too.

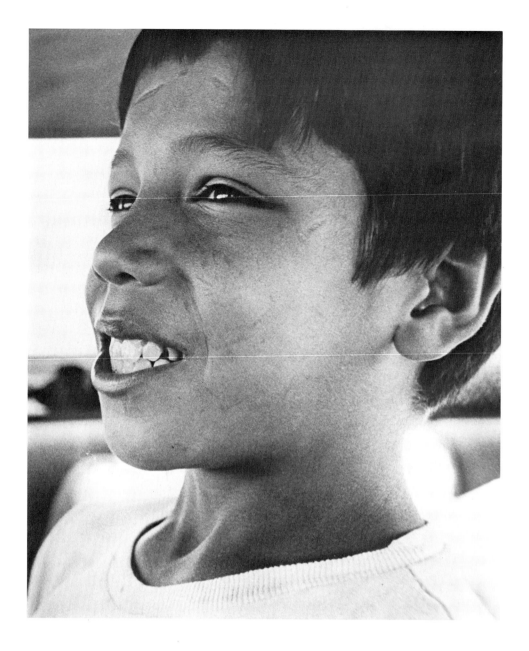

My name is Kevin Wayne Cloud.

I was born on Thanksgiving Day in Cook County Hospital in Chicago. I suddenly popped out and started flying around the room. Mama says she doubts that I flew, but I did.

I like to tease like that. I tease everybody. Sometimes when I tease Mama she pretends to beat me up. I like that.

I'm ten, but I've already got a lot of scars. Mama calls them my growing up scars. Once I fell when I was a baby. Another time a kid threw a bottle at me, and last year a kid at school pushed me against a desk.

I'm an Indian, an American Indian. My family belongs to the Chippewa tribe. We live in the city.

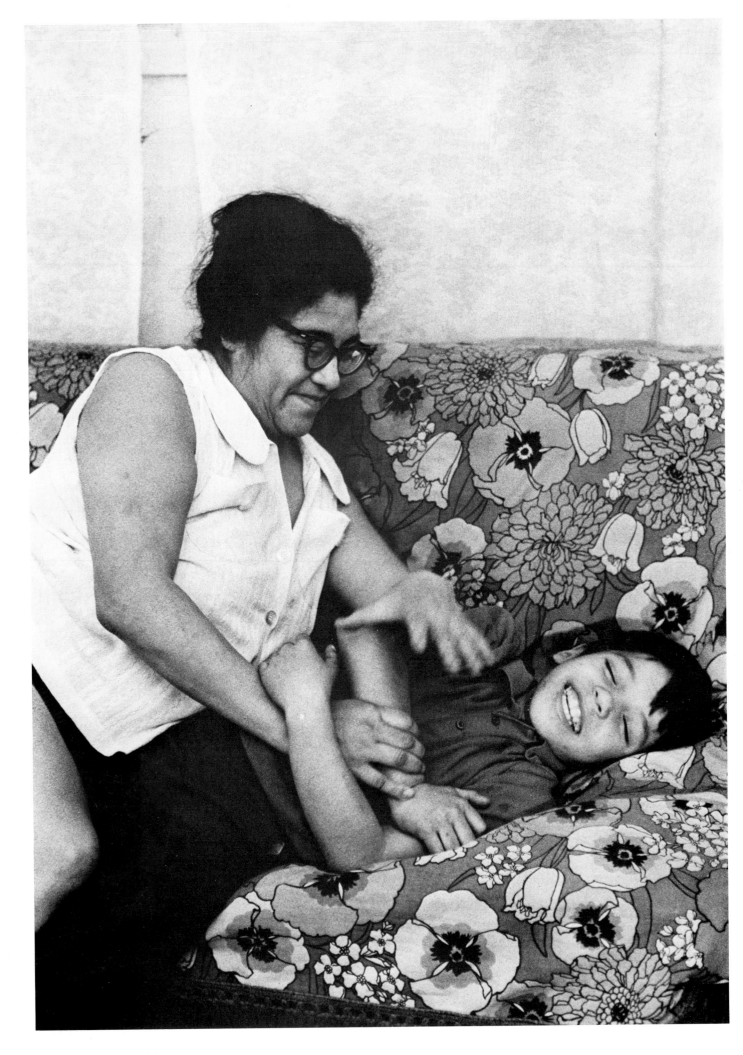

I've got two older sisters, Sheila and Brenda, and a little brother, Mark. Then there's Dino, our dog. And Joey, our cat—and Mama. My uncle Obe lives with us, too, and Grandma. But they're not in the picture.

We got Dino from a neighbor. He was funny looking. Sometimes we play football with Dino. Me and my friends. Mostly he chases us and we tackle him. But we let him make a touchdown every once in a while so he won't feel bad.

My father doesn't live with us. I haven't seen him in a long time.

I have four aunts and another uncle besides Obe, and ten cousins. They all live close to us in Uptown in Chicago. A lot of Indian people live in Uptown.

One of my favorite games is blindman's bluff. Most of the time we play in the park. But sometimes we play in the vacant lot next door. I like to play in the park better because you don't have to watch out for broken bottles and stuff.

Grandma likes to play blindman's bluff. She says she remembers playing it when she was a little girl at Indian boarding school. She plays baseball with us, too, sometimes. Once she slid into home plate. That was funny.

Grandma babysits with Mark and my two little cousins while Mama and my aunt are at work.

Mark, he's always busy hunting for bugs. Grandma says, "That bug will bite you." Mark says, "I'm not afraid. I'll shoot him with my gun." But Mark's really mixed up. He calls flies *cockroaches*.

Mama and Grandma and the rest of my family used to live in Cass Lake, Minnesota. On Leech Lake Reservation. Mama says there were no jobs there and no places to go. She came to Chicago before I was born.

Grandma says the Chippewa have lived on Leech Lake for a long, long time. There's an old story, a legend, about how the Chippewa came to live in Minnesota. My grandfather used to tell it.

The Great Spirit sent a crane to fly across the sky and find a place for the Chippewa to live. As he flew over one lake, Lake Superior, he gave out a loud cry. And he was answered by a loon. A loon is a bird. So the crane knew that it was a good place to live.

My grandfather belonged to the Loon clan, and so Mama is a member of the Loon clan, too. A clan is like a big family. I'm not a member of any clan because my father was white. My last name is Cloud because Mama took her old name back when my father left.

I don't have a real Indian name, but Brenda does. She was born in Cass Lake. They had a naming ceremony for her up there. Her Indian name is something like C-Kwa-Duke. But she doesn't ever use it. She says nobody could spell it or say it.

Grandma speaks Indian. Mama does, too, and all my aunts and uncles. I understand a few words. Grandma tries to teach us.

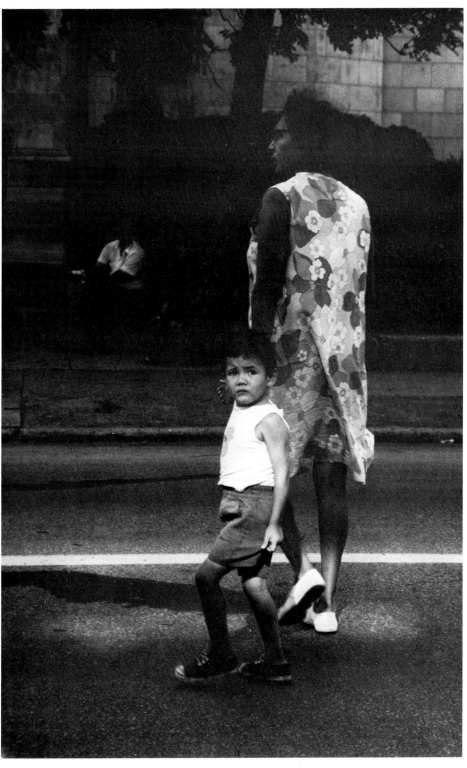

Grandma goes to the Episcopal church. I was baptized by that
church, but I don't go very often. I like to sleep on Sunday mornings.
I'm a sleepyhead.

Obe sleeps in the daytime, too, but he works at night.
He used to work for a carnival. He traveled a lot. But now he lives
with us and works out of the daily pay office. They send him to work
in a factory in the suburbs.

Brenda works out of the daily pay office, too, on Christmas
vacation and other vacations when she wants to earn money
for clothes.

Mama works at the Montrose Urban Progress Center. They're
supposed to help people find jobs. She keeps records. She says
it's hard work.

Grandma is always going to powwows. I go once in a while. When we went to a powwow last summer, Grandma wore a Chippewa dress that she made. She has five Indian dresses. Three are Chippewa with beadwork. The other two have ribbons. A Winnebago lady made them. Winnebagos are a different tribe.

I wore some Indian moccasins from Cass Lake and danced the rabbit dance.

Grandma helped cook and serve. The Indian food we had was fry bread and hominy. But I liked the fried chicken best. That's one of my favorite foods. Grandma gave me a nice piece.

It was cold that night, and they started a big fire that we could sit around to keep warm. They danced for a long time. Grandma said it was a real good powwow that night.

I'd rather go to powwows than go to school.

I don't like school so much. We tease for fun, but the kids at school tease to be mean. They tease us because we're Indians. Last year some kids chased Sheila and me and some of my cousins. They wanted to beat Sheila up. They were too big for us to fight, so we ran up to where Mama works.

Mama was mad. She took off work and went to school the next day. The ones who chased us got in trouble. The principal suspended them, and Grandma started walking us home from school. I hated school last year.

Mama says we're going to move when Brenda gets out of high school because it's getting too rough around here. I don't know where we'll move to.

Mama says she hopes I finish school, but she's afraid I won't because I'm a boy. I guess she thinks boys always think of something better to do or get into fights or something. My sister Brenda, she's got scholarships for four years of college. She wants to be a social worker. I haven't decided what I'll be.

The first thing I do when I get home from school is get out my bike. I like to ride my bike more than anything else. I ride a lot with my cousin Myron. Myron's nine. He lives down the street. I ride with Andy, too. He lives upstairs. But Andy doesn't have a lock and chain. Myron does.

When I ride with Myron, we stop and lock our bikes together. Myron pins the key to his shirt so he won't lose it. When Myron isn't around I bring my bike in. It would get stolen otherwise. I bring it in when my legs get tired.

Myron and me, we go everywhere. Mama says, "That Kevin, he really gets around, he knows more people than I do."

Sometimes we go down to Lincoln Park Zoo and to the North Avenue Beach. Once we went almost all the way downtown. Myron didn't know his way home, but I did. We always stay on this side of Broadway. The colored kids might beat us up if we went across Broadway.

Last summer we went up to the reservation in Minnesota to harvest wild rice and to visit Aunt Rose. She's Mama's cousin. It was a long way. I kept asking how much further it was. At first I said I wasn't going because I'd miss the Friday night movie on TV.

I was little when I was in Minnesota the last time, and I didn't remember much. We don't go up very often. It's too far. And we don't have a car. An Indian man drove us up last summer. Grandma has gone up more times. She pointed out things on the way. Once she pointed out the Chippewa River.

Mark kept getting into trouble whenever we stopped. He always does. And Mama kept telling Sheila, "Go get Mark." But sometimes Sheila wouldn't and then Mama would tell her she was selfish.

There are many birch trees on the path to the place on the lake where
Aunt Rose launched her boat. Grandma says the place was an old
Indian campsite. And not everybody knew about it. She says she
remembers when they used to camp there before white men harvested
wild rice or made rules about it.

The old Chippewa used the bark from the white birch trees to

make canoes, to cover their wigwams, and for rice trays and sugar baskets. They knew how to strip the bark from the trees without killing them. Grandma says she used to watch my great-grandfather making canoes. She says everybody who knew how to make them is probably dead, and besides, it's hard to get the wood. That's why they don't make them now.

It rained the first day of ricing. But Aunt Rose said that wouldn't make any difference. Everybody got up early. We saw many cars with boats on top. Each time an Indian went by, Grandma said, "There goes an Indian to rice." But if it was a white man, she didn't say anything. Only Indians and people who live on the reservation are allowed to rice, but a lot of white people live on the reservation.

Most Indians don't have their own boats. Aunt Rose rented her
boat from a white man. She had to sell her rice to him. She also bought
a license and a pair of knockers. Knockers are long wooden sticks.
They use them to knock the rice into the boat.

Aunt Rose dropped some tobacco in the water before she started
ricing. Mama says that's the old Indian way of giving thanks for the
rice. The old religion is called Midewiwin.

Aunt Rose lives in a house in the town of Cass Lake. My cousin and me, we had a dirt fight there. That was fun. Before we left, Mama bought some wild rice at the store. We usually have white rice at home. Mama says the wild rice you buy in Chicago doesn't taste right, and it costs too much money.

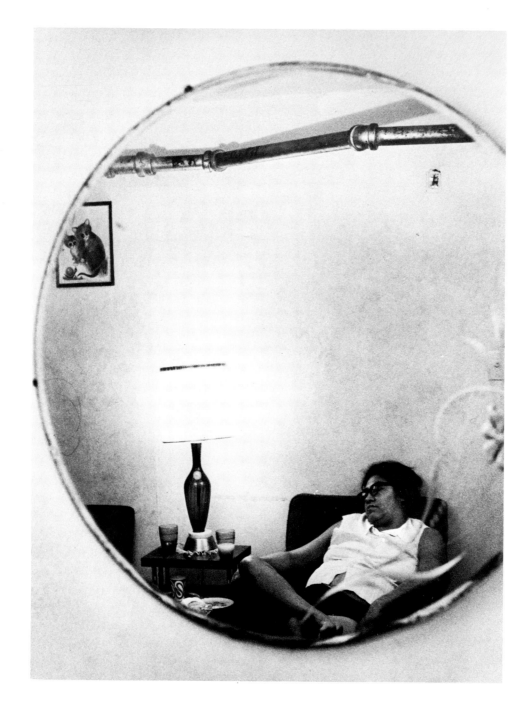

We were all tired when we got back. Mama fell asleep. She falls asleep in the chair a lot, but she says she doesn't. We tease her, and then she says, "Well, open that window and I won't fall asleep." But she does anyway.

I found a little kitten in the street. Mama said to take it into the house. But Dino and Joey didn't like it, so we couldn't keep it.

I started pestering Mama to let me have a birthday party 'cause my tenth birthday was coming up. She said she'd think about it. Brenda said, "Why don't you let him have a party?"

Myron, Bryant, and Little Kevin came to my birthday party.
Little Kevin is shorter than me. That's why they call him Little Kevin.
Stephanie was supposed to come, but she got sick. She's another one
of my cousins. I don't like girls so much. They chase me and try
to kiss me. But Stephanie is okay.

For my party we ate hot dogs and cake. Grandma made some
hominy. I always help her cut off the corn. She made a lot, but it

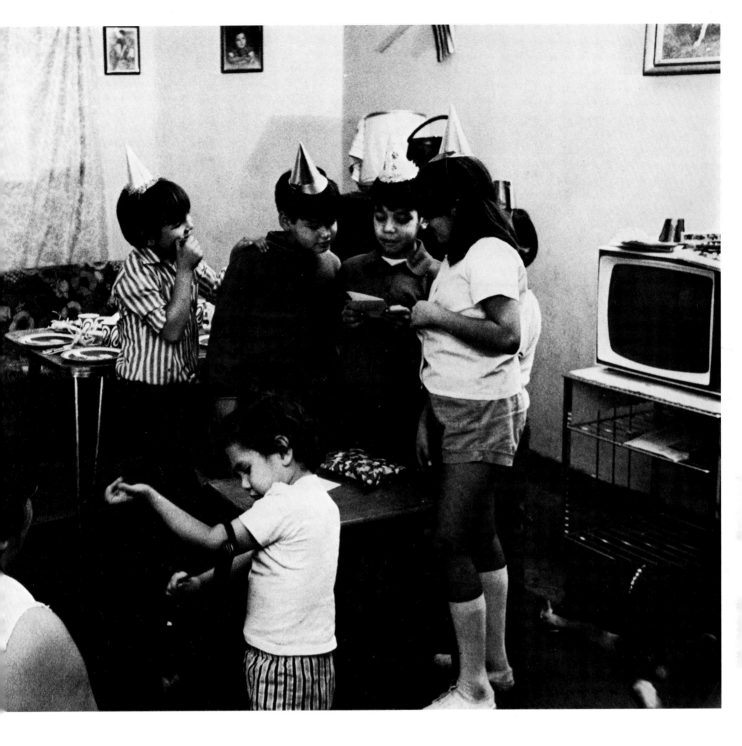

didn't last long. My aunts all came over to get some. They all like Grandma's hominy.

I got a lot of presents. Some money, long underwear from Mama, a gun that shoots corks, and a rodeo set. I also got some little cars, but Mark broke them. Sometimes I think you can't keep anything around here.

After I opened my presents we went outside. It was my first birthday party. I'll probably remember it a long time.

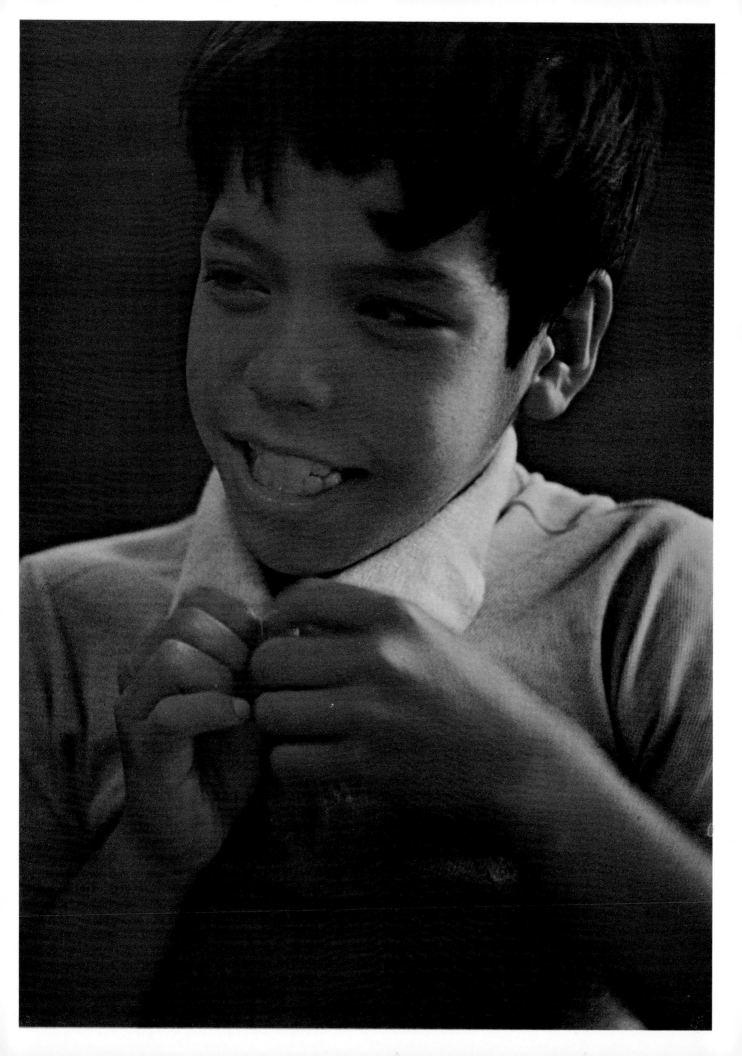

Words in Kevin's World

Birch trees have a flaky looking bark that peels off easily. It is called *birchbark*, and the Chippewa used it to make their houses, canoes, and many other things that they needed.

Blindman's bluff, or *buff*, is a game that American Indians played many years ago. It is one of the games that Indians taught to white people.

Chippewa is the English word for a tribe, or group, of American Indians whose home for many years has been the area near Lake Superior, Lake Michigan, and Lake Huron. The Indian name for the tribe is *Ojibway*. The Chippewa are a *Woodland* tribe—they lived in the woods and were fine hunters and fishermen. Some also had gardens. They used their canoes to travel the many lakes and rivers of their land.

A *clan* is a group of families who are descended from the same ancestor. Kevin's mother belongs to the Loon clan, which was the clan of her father. Among the Chippewa a child becomes a member of the clan to which his or her father belongs.

At a *daily pay office*, people can get work for one day at a time. The office sends workers to factories in the suburbs and other places that need extra help. There are many daily pay offices in Uptown, where Kevin lives, and many American Indians find work through them. But the pay is not very good.

Hominy is an Indian word for a food that is made by boiling dried squaw corn, or Indian corn, in water. Squaw corn is the colorful corn that is sometimes used as a Thanksgiving decoration.

Indian boarding school is a government school for American Indian children. The children live at the school, away from their families.

Indian names, such as Brenda's name, C-Kwa-Duke, were given to Chippewa children when they showed that they were ready to learn the ways of their tribe. Each child had his or her own special name. Most American Indians use first and last names today.

Knockers are a pair of long wooden sticks that the Chippewa use to harvest wild rice. A knocker in one hand is used to bend the rice stalks over the boat. The other knocker is used to beat the grains of rice off the stalks and into the boat.

Legends are very old stories that older people tell the children of a tribe. Telling legends is an Indian way of teaching children about life.

A *loon* is a black bird that looks like a duck. It lives near water and eats fish. The loon has a strange, laughing call that can be heard from far away.

Midewiwin is the Indian name for the Chippewa religion. Some members of the Midewiwin Society, a special group, treated people who were sick. Each tribe had its own religion, but all the Indian religions respected the things of nature. Many American Indians have become Christians, but some still believe in the old religion.

Powwow is an Indian word for a feast, dance, or a public meeting. It is now a part of the American language, and it means an important discussion.

In the *rabbit dance* the dancers try to move like rabbits. This dance is just one of many Chippewa dances. Until about a hundred years ago the Chippewa danced as part of their religion. Today most Indian dancing is done for fun.

Reservations are areas of land that are supposed to be set aside for use by American Indians. Long ago, the United States government and the Indian tribes signed agreements, or treaties, that promised the land to the Indians.

A *tribe* is a large group of American Indians who speak the same language, share the same customs, and usually have the same leaders. The Chippewa tribe was made up of many clans. At one time 300 different Indian tribes lived in America.

Kevin lives in *Uptown,* an area of Chicago that is about one mile square. Around 10,000 American Indians live in Uptown, as well as black, Puerto Rican, and some white families.

Wigwam is the name for the kind of house the Chippewa once used. Wigwams were made by bending tree limbs and covering them with birchbark. The houses were round and could be put up in one day.

Wild rice is a grass that grows in some lakes and rivers. The Chippewa harvested the grain of this grass. It was one of their main foods along with wild game and fish, maple sugar, and wild berries.

Winnebago is the name of an Indian tribe. Winnebagos were neighbors of the Chippewa tribe.